COLLEGE OF MARIN LIBRARY
KENTFIELD, CALIFORNIA

S0-BLK-861

WITHDRAWN

Style in Pottery

other books by the author

———

Dish, tin-glazed earthenware painted in high-temperature colours.
ENGLAND (LIVERPOOL); about 1760. W. 13 in.
Victoria and Albert Museum

Style in Pottery

ARTHUR LANE

NK
4225
L3
1974

NOYES PRESS

Park Ridge, New Jersey 07656, U.S.A.

Copyright © 1974 by Angela Lane
Library of Congress Catalog Card Number: 73-85181
ISBN: 0-8155-5025-1
Printed in Great Britain

Published in the United States by
NOYES PRESS
Noyes Building
Park Ridge, New Jersey 07656

Preface

The original edition of this book came out in 1948. Nothing to compare with it has appeared before or since, and it has seemed well worth while to re-issue it in its present format. In so personal a book it would have been an impertinence to tamper with the text, and in consequence nothing has been done beyond correcting one or two plain mistakes which slipped through the net in the first edition, and adding one coloured and a few monochrome illustrations. Care has been taken to select only subjects which are known to have found favour with the author in his lifetime.

R. J. CHARLESTON

Contents

Introduction

QUITE apart from the needs that make it a part of their everyday lives, most people regard pottery with friendly feelings, gladly including quite a lot of it among the not strictly useful objects that help to turn a dwelling into a home. But on the whole they are indulgently uncritical about the aesthetic qualities of these possessions. Pictures and furniture are readily defended as the expression of personal taste, but 'china' is something that just happens. It may acquire a special sanctity if identified (by an 'expert') as Worcester, Wedgwood, or Dresden; yet even the experts, the collectors, tend to sharpen their appreciation only so far as to distinguish between the work of different factories. If asked to explain the value of their favourite pieces, considered purely as works of art, most collectors would treat the question as unfair and irrelevant.

But the potters who for thousands of years have served the human race have for the most part been intelligent craftsmen, consciously exercising a complicated ritual to turn out a decent job. Many have possessed an intuitive gift that enabled them to go farther, to impose on serviceable vessels that element of willed fantasy that we describe as 'style'; these have in fact been artists. Not necessarily artists in the modern individualistic sense, for the finest pottery has often been the product less of an individual than a team, a whole workshop whose collective experience took more than a generation or two to ripen. Pottery, whether regarded as art or craft, has limits to its range of expression; it is naturally measured by the grasp of a pair of hands; it is dominated by the circular section of the wheel; even when purely ornamental, it tends to preserve the convention of being an utensil. Surely, then, within these limits it must be possible to discover some constant principles, to which the imaginative vagaries of pottery style must in varying degree conform.

This book attempts to discover such principles. But it remains for the reader to test them by first-hand knowledge of actual specimens. No photographic illustrations, however good, can do more than suggest the delights of colour, texture, and volume through which pottery makes its most direct appeal. And though there is pottery of some kind always around us, most of it is confined within the modern idiom of industrial white porcelain or earthenware, and we may be confused by the innumerable modern reproductions in earlier styles. A widely critical judgement is best formed by study of the selected pieces in museums, where alone we are likely to see wares of all periods and civilizations. Even within the range of a single period or factory we may need to see several vessels together before we become fully conscious of their common 'style'.

February 1948   ARTHUR LANE

The Potter's Means and Aims

By 'pottery' let us here mean vessels of baked clay, complete in themselves, and not images of living things. We thus rule out decorated tilework, which is a part of architecture, and pottery or porcelain figures, which could be considered as sculpture. 'Style' will mean good handling of potter's material —not necessarily the 'style' of a particular epoch in art-history, such as we understand by Gothic, Renaissance, and so on. For though potters in every age share some ideas of form and decoration with workers in other materials, they can express those ideas only so far as their control over their pottery medium allows. Coarse pottery is easy enough to make; but refinements of texture, surface, and ornament call for a fund of technical knowledge that can only be acquired by long experiment or by learning from other potters who have already mastered the problem. Knowledge of this kind may be handed down through generations, and transmitted from one country to another either by wandering potters or by examples of their work. An instance familiar to all is the painted porcelain of China, which reached Europe in such quantities during the seventeenth and eighteenth centuries. European potters took a long time to discover how true porcelain was made, but both before and after the discovery they successfully imitated the shapes and decoration of the Chinese wares, though these were completely at variance with the idiom of European art. Nothing could illustrate more clearly the working of the potter's mind. He is absorbed first and foremost with the technical mysteries of his craft, and is prepared to accept as incidentals whatever forms and decoration are proposed by his teacher, who may live at the opposite end of the world. The novelty of the new technique must wear off before he can regard it simply as a means for expressing the artistic ideas of his own society.

We as laymen are naturally most interested in the appearance of the finished pot. When we begin to analyse our reasons for liking it or not, we think first of its shape, then of the skill evident in arranging and carrying out the decoration. These are, so to speak, intellectual qualities, not too hard to explain in words. But when we come to such things as colour, roughness or smoothness of surface, and solidity or flimsiness of the clay material, then words are harder to find. For these are sensuous qualities; they ruffle the surface of our emotions in the most pleasing way; but how can we describe their value to people who have not undergone the same experience? Western writers on ceramics borrow homely metaphors from cookery; the Chinese more poetically compare the appearance of a glaze to phenomena in nature, such as 'blue of the sky after rain'. However indescribable, the sensuous qualities are more important in pottery than in almost any other minor art. The very material of which a pot is made is part of its 'style'.

Not all clays are suitable material for the potter. Some are not stiff enough to bear modelling; others crack or melt in the fire. It is usually necessary to mix two or more kinds of clay, sand, or powdered rock, after each has been thoroughly cleansed. The kinds of clay used, and the carefully regulated ascending degree of heat in the kiln, both help to determine the texture of the finished pots; whether they are to be earthenware, relatively soft and loosely knit; stoneware, dense, hard, and heavy; or porcelain, which is harder than stoneware, brilliantly white, and translucent where the walls of the pot

are thin. Porcelain is one of the most beautiful artificial sub-
stances that man can make, and stoneware has a ringing
integrity that sets it high above soft earthenware.

Liquids will soak through earthenware unless it is protected
by glaze, which is in effect a thin surface coat of glass. Glazes
for earthenware are usually made of finely ground sand or
quartz mixed in water with a 'flux'—potash, soda, oxide of
lead; the flux causes the mixture to melt and fuse itself on to
the clay while the temperature in the kiln is comparatively low.
Stoneware and porcelain are impervious to liquids, but gain
a pleasanter surface when glazed. A peculiar glaze can be
formed on stoneware by throwing common salt into the kiln
when the heat is greatest; this causes the surface of the pot
itself to vitrify, but also disintegrates it into a pebbled texture
like that of an orange-skin. Other laid-on glazes for stoneware
can be made of clay or powdered stones mixed with a flux.
On porcelain the glaze is of flux and china-stone, the felspathic
rock that with china clay forms the composition of the porcelain itself; here the physical union of glaze and pot is complete.

Colour is the most potent magic the potter can command.
Allied with glaze, it may have a freshness and luminosity
unattainable in any other medium of art, and this freshness
does not fade with time. All potter's colours have to pass
through fire, and for that reason they must be of mineral
origin—oxides of iron, copper, cobalt, and so on. Dyes from
plants or insects (madder or cochineal, for example) will not
do. It is the action of the fire itself that transmutes these
drab-looking minerals into the bright colours on the finished
pot. Sometimes colouring matter is mixed with the glaze; or
a clear glaze may allow colours underneath to show through;
or painting in colours may be added over the fired glaze, in
which case the pot must be sent to the kiln once again. Some
of the potter's finest effects are those of broken colour, caused

by the interaction of fire, molten glaze, and underlying clay.

Such then, in bare outline, are the potter's materials—clay 'body', glaze, and colours. They are hardly 'raw' materials, for they must be so carefully worked on before they are fit to use. The uninstructed layman sees nothing of the immense labour in applied chemistry and physics by which a glaze or body is prepared. But he will often recognize traces of the ordeal the pots have gone through in the fire. The body may have sagged slightly out of shape; the glaze may have run unevenly in waves or drops, leaving parts of the clay exposed; colours, too, may be uneven in tone, and painted decoration may have blurred in the swimming glaze. Should we condemn these accidents as flaws? Not without asking what the potter was aiming at, and to what extent he claimed to control them. A defect in pottery made with the mechanical resources of modern industry cannot be excused. And a high standard of technical perfection is demanded of any potter who seeks the refined effects proper to such an exquisite material as porcelain. But to many other kinds of pottery a casual roughness gives the breath of life. Fire is an awe-inspiring, unaccountable element, and it is good that this wild partner should at times assert his share in the potter's work. But then the human contribution, the shape and ornament of the pot, must be correspondingly robust. When the two forces act in harmony, as they did so often in China and the Near East, the resulting wares have a power to stir the imagination seldom encountered in European pottery.

A potter can give shape to his wet clay in various ways. He can pinch out a small bowl or build up a large vase with his unaided hands. To save walking round the vase he could turn it on a pivoted disk, or slow wheel. But this primitive instrument was replaced as soon as might be by the fast-revolving potter's wheel, which caused the clay to spring up inside the potter's hands under its own power. The wheel to this day dominates pottery shape. It is true that in Roman times, in the eighteenth century, and in our modern industrial potteries clay vessels have commonly been shaped by pressing in moulds. But at some stage these moulded pieces are almost invariably transferred to the wheel or lathe, either for trimming or for decoration. And in consequence the horizontal section of most pots is a circle. The potter may indent the circle with fluting or draw it out into lobes while the clay is still soft (e.g. Plates 15 and 19), but he usually expresses his sense of form through the vertical curves, angles, and straight lines of the vessel seen in profile. These admit of astonishing variety. They are affected by the texture and the plastic strength of the wet clay. Delicate mouldings would be inappropriate if the clay were coarse-grained, and with some clays extravagant curves would invite collapse. There is a direct relationship between the curves of a vase, the thickness of its walls, and the strength of the clay; and 'good potting' allows the clay to reveal its strength by making the walls no thicker than they need be to support the shape.

Soft clay on the wheel seems of itself to suggest certain shapes to the potter's hand. All are based on the sphere, the ovoid, the cone, and the cylinder. Some pots even when finished record each intuitive gesture of their maker (Plate 24). But usually the potter's spontaneity must yield something to the material demand for use, or the spiritual demand for elaboration. A storage jar need only be rough, but vessels to eat and drink from should be smooth for cleanliness and comfort in handling. Smoothness, a primary aim of potters from the earliest times, draws attention away from the volume and substance of a vase to concentrate on its profile outlines. The handles and spouts so often necessary to household wares yet further detract from the roundness of the shape; one is

almost compelled to look at the pot from one or other of two
opposite sides. Now nothing could be more insipid than a pot
in which we are aware of the two-dimensional outlines alone,
with an uninteresting neutral area in the middle. The very first
problem the potter as artist has to solve is how to reaffirm
the third dimension, the bulge of the shape between the two
profiles to right and left. He can do it in the simplest way by
modifying the shape. Let us at this point observe the crucial
part played in pottery form by horizontal lines. From the way
our bodies are constructed, the most reassuring sight in nature,
the orientation by which we gauge space and form in relation
to ourselves, is the horizontal line—the line of our two eyes, of
the horizon. We have an exact and immediate perception of
length when the lines are cut short—we measure them from
the centre outwards. As any dress designer knows, such lines
are best avoided in fashions for the full figure. But they are
very serviceable to the potter. For if in turning the pot he
makes ridges or grooves, these will become horizontal lines
bridging the space between the profiles and tying them together. A sharp kink in the profile will have almost the same
effect. And our eyes cannot help but measure these lines; they
explore out from the centre and back again, with a subconscious
muscular action that at once makes us aware of the receding
curves of the pot. How true this is Plates 13 and 40 will show.
It is a favourite trick to concentrate these measurable horizontal
lines round the narrower parts of the pot, towards the neck or
foot; they there give a sense of constriction that emphasizes
the free escape of the curves between them (Plates 5, 11 and
17). One might go so far as to say that no pot shape appears
really stable unless it has at least one strongly defined horizontal accent. Most often its place is the foot or lip (or both),
but Plate 1 shows a shape that is slung from the line of the
shoulder.

[16]

In using such words as lip, neck, shoulder, belly to describe the shape of a pot we acknowledge its likeness to a living thing. Potters have at various times emphasized the idea by giving animal or vegetable shape to part of a vessel, if not the whole. In the Chelsea vase, Plate 34, the suggestion of life is the more disturbing because not explicit; a metamorphosis appears to have been arrested just before reaching the shape of any animal we know. But beyond this point pottery begins to encroach upon sculpture. Its true genius, like that of architecture, is closely bound up with abstract geometrical form.

The potter can suggest volume in ways other than by modifying the shape. He can do it through ornament on the surface of the pot. It hardly matters whether the ornament is carved, moulded, or painted, though each technique has its own problems, its own possibilities for delight. Nor can we say that some subjects are suitable for pottery-decoration and others not; the mythological figure-painting on early Greek vases is just as legitimate as the casually ornamental abstracts from nature so dear to the Chinese. Everything depends on the way the decoration is spaced, on the extent to which it emphasizes the shape and roundness of the pot. We may distinguish three principal rhythms in pottery ornament; the single punctuation mark that first seizes our attention; the continuous frieze that leads our eye in imagination right round the pot; and the all-over repeating pattern, which again suggests continuity where the motives narrow out in perspective to right and left. The vase in Plate 38 shows with classic simplicity the leaping fish as punctuation, the painted horizontal bands below and above as continuous frieze. The potter has here so reduced the importance of lip and foot that we first apprehend the shape and volume of the pot through following the suggestions offered by the painting. Other good examples of 'punctuation' are seen in Plates 5, 20, and 37; of

B

continuous frieze in Plates 4, 9, 17, and 34; of all-over design in Plates 11 and 18. Ornament, to be successful, should gracefully beckon our attention to other qualities of the pot. It fails if through over-elaboration or over-emphasis it prevents us from noticing anything else.

Very often the surface to be decorated is that of a shallow plate or dish. Here there is no third dimension to think of, and the decorator has greater scope. Dishes have often been designed as show-pieces, to stand on edge against a wall. Some have a very definite 'right way up' for the picture on them. But even so one cannot help feeling that the most satisfactory designs are those which emphasize the circularity of the shape, whether by a continuous border, by radiating or 'all-over' patterns, or by a 'punctuation-mark' arrangement comprehensible from any point of view (Plates 9, 10, 12, 22, 28, and 31).

We have now considered material, shapes, and ornament, leaving a less obvious but still important point till last. At all times the main bulk of pottery has been made for household use. This in itself imposes conditions on style—we have noticed smoothness, handles, and spouts. Now pottery, like other utensils, can be perfectly adapted for use and at the same time hideous to look at. Before the Second World War there was much talk of 'functionalism' in the useful arts. Its promoters used this catchword to discredit the fripperies of their predecessors and open the way for new fripperies of their own. But many simple people were deceived: at last, they thought, this incomprehensible nonsense called art can be explained away: usefulness and beauty are the same thing. Years of shabby living may now have taught them to think again. Usefulness is no more than a condition to be fulfilled. Grace in fulfilment is an extra, properly called art. In pottery it may go no farther than a choice of certain proportions in shape, backed by good material competently used. But usually men's imagination has craved for something more, and potters have been able and willing to give it them. How far ornament or elaboration should go depends on appetite. A point is reached where usefulness and elaboration begin to conflict; the pottery has to be used with special care, perhaps only on special occasions; it becomes an instrument of ceremony. The care may be worth while; people consent to wear special uncomfortable clothes for parties, because this heightens their sense of importance. The fine porcelain of the eighteenth century would have spiritual advantages over the canteen mug, even if one had to wash up oneself. Finally, pottery may reach a point where it is of no 'use' at all, except to be looked at, like a painting or sculpture. And why not, if we like looking at pottery? Feeding, ceremony, and contemplation are all legitimate human activities, and in each the potter can serve us well.

The Ancient World

FROM the beginnings of human civilization to the fall of the Western Roman Empire is a very long time, and it might seem hard to find any common factor in pottery made during some five thousand years. But there is one; for except in Egypt and Mesopotamia, the use of vitreous glaze was almost unknown to the Ancient World. A rather soft red, buff, or grey earthenware was the only medium in which the potters of Pre-Dynastic Egypt, Classical Greece, and Imperial Rome could express their styles. It was a meagre material. And there was only a limited and sober range of colourings to help it out; orange-reds, browns, and blacks from iron in the clay; some purple, and some white that could be laid on as matt over-all washes or painted designs. Among backward peoples these simple materials are used to this day.

The good workmanship and strong sense of style shown by some prehistoric pottery appears astonishing. But then, pottery was about the finest thing these people could make, and it therefore claimed the best of their skill. Even without the help of a potter's wheel they could produce shapes whose irregularity is almost unnoticeable. Many pots have rounded or pointed bottoms that look to us unstable, but set in the scooped-out hollow of an uneven earth floor they would be as steady as a sitting hen. As for decoration, the most obvious method was to indent patterns by hand or with simple tools in the wet clay itself, and a good example is the wavy band of finger-marks on the Persian storage-jar, Plate I. But apart from

I

2

3

4

its convenience, a smooth surface gave prehistoric man an aesthetic satisfaction that we can still understand when we look at his polished stone vases and axe-heads to-day. Pottery was often burnt black, or coated with a wash of soapy red clay, and then burnished bright with a stone until it looked like polished stone itself (e.g. Plate 2). Earthenware thus treated almost transcends its material limitations.

But these limitations were felt, and we may perhaps regard painting on pottery as a device to draw attention away from them. Without its admirable frieze of painted birds the Peruvian pot in Plate 3 would be a dull object. And the Ancient Greek potters seem to have regarded the bare surface of their clay as a negative quantity, to be replaced as far as possible by a closely integrated sheath of painted ornament. One feels this very strongly in the Iron Age jug, Plate 4. From the seventh to the fifth centuries B.C. the Greeks refined the old earthenware materials to the limit of what was possible, and in particular developed a glossy black pigment produced by the differential action of fire on a wash of clay, disintegrated into its finest elements by an admixture of potash. This was not a glaze; it did not melt in the fire; and it retained the sharpness of the painter's touch. Glaze should soften painting on or under it; it always softens the outline of a pot by filling in the angles and depressions. Perhaps the early Greeks would have rejected the sensuous attractions of glaze even had it been available. For their own intellectual temperament demanded the utmost clarity of form and drawing (Plates 5 and 6). They pared down the walls of a vase on the wheel to the most exact curves and angles—no other pottery is so certain in its profiles. The geometric element always present in wheel-made wares is here exploited to give an extraordinary sense of vital tension, akin to that we recognize in the lines of a high-speed aircraft. It is supremely unnatural, something conceived in the human mind without reference to the outer world. Unnatural, too, are the stylized plant-forms, the palmettes and lotuses of the painted decoration. The Greek artist had eyes for the human figure alone. Here is no place to consider the exquisite detail of Greek figure-painting; we may only remark how aptly it was used to emphasize the most important part of the pot; how well it was fitted into a complicated structure of painted ornament stretching continuously over the clay surface, with vertical and horizontal accents always related to the members of the shape. Before their art fell into decline, the Greek vase-painters always showed their figures as flat profiles standing on a single ground-line, without any suggestion of depth or perspective. In fact, they followed a golden rule that holds good for all painting on pottery; no excess of modelling or recession should break through the continuity of the surface; no ideas of space should be allowed to compete with the volume of the pot, which itself supplies all that is needed of the third dimension.

When this rule was regularly broken, pottery soon fell into discredit as a serious form of Greek art. The best the later Greek and Roman potters could do was to imitate, in a baser material, the embossed designs on vessels of metal. But on the outskirts of the Roman world there were signs of new vitality. For example, the very unclassical-looking jar from Britain, Plate 7A, is painted in thick white clay slip—a curious anticipation of the later Staffordshire technique (compare Plates 25 and 26B). And the Egypto-Roman cup of Plate 7B, though in shape directly copied from a silver one, is covered with coloured glazes, green outside and yellow within. It is a definite link with the great development of glazed wares in medieval Islam.

The Near East

WHILE Europe passed into its Dark Ages a new civilization of great material splendour was already flowering
in Muhammedan Asia. And about the beginning of the
ninth century A.D. some of the bales of merchandise arriving
at Baghdad contained Chinese porcelain and stoneware. For
the first time pottery stood revealed to the Caliph's court as
a fine art. The Islamic potters now received every encourage-
ment to embark on a career of resourceful experiment in colour
and design that for nine centuries made them formidable
rivals of the Chinese. They were not especially interested in
the texture and mass of their clay, though in the twelfth century
they developed a translucent white composition akin to soft-
paste porcelain. Nor did their pottery shapes, however well
chosen, show much variety or sense of volume—in fact, some
of the finest work went into the flat tiles with which they
decorated the inner and outer walls of buildings. The greatness
of Islamic pottery depends on three things: first, its amazingly
rich, but subdued, colour, whether of glaze or painting: second,
its response to the behaviour of light, reflected from the surface
of a pot, casting faint shadows over its modelled ornament, or
even gleaming through the material itself; and third, the superb
control of interwoven, rhythmic decoration that seems to spread
itself naturally over any surface to which it is applied.

On the ivory-white beaker, Plate 8, colour is confined to a
line of glowing blue at the lip; but below this light is allowed
to make magic. The upper band of plant ornament is cut

right through the sides and filled in, like a traceried window, by thick transparent glaze. In the lower band similar designs are engraved on the surface, showing so faintly under the glaze that they are scarcely visible in the illustration. One must imagine the bowl, Plate 9, filled with water; we gaze into a pellucid, slow-flowing stream, where minnows dart over the gently waving water-weeds. A more formal arrangement of design is seen on the pedestal dish, Plate 10, where so much depends on the spacing; but even here coiling plants have begun to weave about the central figure. They spread all over the Turkish jug, Plate 11, a curtain of cool dark- and light-blue and purple. With such ornament a pot can afford to be some-what loose and unemphatic in shape.

3

The Far East

CHINA'S supremacy in the potter's art is unquestioned; her wares have been sought and treasured in all civilized countries; and potters everywhere have looked to them for inspiration. But there was little promise of this success before the time of the T'ang Emperors (A.D. 618-906), and it was thenceforward attained under peculiarly favourable conditions. For during centuries of settled civilization the Chinese regarded pottery as a form of art that need not be bound by the requirements of common use. Perhaps the majority of pieces that we most admire were intended from the first as ceremonial wares, or as treasures for the contemplation of the connoisseur.

The fundamental peculiarity of Chinese pottery is the respect paid to the hardness and density of the clay material. A good, ringing stoneware was produced even before T'ang times (Plate 13); and later stoneware often approaches the quality of porcelain. White porcelain itself was made from the eighth century onwards, though its greatest development began under the Ming Emperors (1368-1644). These hard materials were covered with glazes equally hard, fired at extremely high temperatures. The stoneware ewer in Plate 14, with its molten glaze running unevenly down over the scored surface, might almost have been produced by a volcanic process of nature. In Sung times (A.D. 960-1279) the favourite grey-green 'celadon' glazes were intentionally made to resemble jade; and the Ming porcelain stem-cup (Plate 20) is like a block of some newly discovered precious stone whose pure whiteness is enhanced by the red fish painted under the glaze.

6A
6B

7A
7B

8

9A

9B

IOA

IOB

II

12

13

14

So various are the shapes of Chinese pottery that it seems hard at first to distinguish any constant preferences. But we soon notice a remarkable absence of handles. Even when present, these are often nothing more than loops through which a cord could be passed, and they tend to slide upwards to the neck or shoulder of a vessel (Plates 13 and 14). The pot is thus allowed to protrude its smooth rotundity unmarred by excrescences. In fact, the Chinese potters had a deep appreciation of globular and ovoid volumes (Plates 13, 17, and 18); and the volume inside a pot was conceived as an expanding force; thrusting the walls outwards into a perfect sphere, threatening to burst upwards and spread like a growing plant. This idea was most strongly expressed in the earlier pots (Plates 14, 15, and 19), but it never quite disappeared even in the tall, elegant shapes of the seventeenth and eighteenth centuries. Many later Chinese pots were built into angular shapes from flat slabs of material, as if to deny the natural laws of the potter's wheel (Plate 21). They might be regarded as a perverse attempt by the sophisticated potter to escape from the toils of his own deepest convictions.

The Chinese derived such pleasure from the quality of their ceramic materials that they often felt no need of added ornament. But it is the genius of Far Eastern painting to portray nature in a few sure strokes, exquisitely placed, and this economy of statement is admirably suited to decoration on pottery. Plant-forms here predominate over all others. However simplified, they retain a sense of organic life. Islamic plant-ornament tends either to harden into quasi-geometrical, balanced groups, or else to follow a continuously undulating rhythm. In the Far East this rhythm is often deliberately broken into staccato passages, and the plants form themselves into asymmetrical masses poised against empty space (Plate 22). No feature of Chinese art impressed itself more on

[41]

European consciousness than this studied asymmetry, which, since the eighteenth century, has become firmly acclimatized among our own pottery conventions (compare Plates 31 and 33).

4

Pre-industrial Europe

POTTERY as an art went under in Europe during the early Middle Ages, and its re-emergence from the thirteenth century onwards was painfully slow. It is indeed possible to trace a continuous tradition from that time to the present day, but overlaid on this are two alien traditions, borrowed respectively from the Islamic World and from the Far East.

Late Gothic potters in England and France worked in soft earthenware with a glossy lead-glaze. This could only be decorated by manipulating the clay, or by trailing on patterns in clay 'slip' of a different colour. Rustic potters were still making 'slipware' in the seventeenth and eighteenth centuries; as Plate 25 shows, it had a thoroughly earthy character, and a clumsiness in shape due partly to the thick lead-glaze. The Germans had already discovered a superior material—hard stoneware. In the tall tankard, Plate 24, this is unglazed: in fact here we have wheel-made pottery in its most elementary form, a petrified record of the potter's first motions in 'throwing' a lump of clay. Later German stoneware was covered with a film of 'salt-glaze' so thin as not to obscure the finely moulded relief-patterns with which it was normally decorated. Towards the end of the seventeenth century potters in England began making not only salt-glazed stoneware of German type, but also a highly fired unglazed red ware suggested by imported Chinese pieces like the tea-pot in Plate 23. Freed from the use of lead-glaze, which had clogged up all fine detail of shape and modelling, they soon discovered a new finesse in handling their

clay. Plates 26A and 27 show successive stages in sensibility
to form. Though the easy rusticity of the old slipware per-
sisted in much Staffordshire pottery of the eighteenth century
(e.g. Plate 26B), the salt-glaze jug in Plate 27 already shows
a cleanness of outline, a neat precision of handle and lip, that
foreshadows the later accomplishments of Josiah Wedgwood.
It was he who improved Staffordshire material into the famous
cream-coloured 'Queen's ware' (Plate 35), which has almost
the delicacy of porcelain and is far cheaper to make on an
industrial scale. Wedgwood shared the interest of his day in
the Ancient Greek pottery then recently discovered in Italy,
and he introduced something of Greek clarity into the outlines
of his own wares. But his style owes as much to the native
Staffordshire craftsmanship, and to a keen appreciation of
modern practical needs. In fact, a hard white ware of Wedgwood type is that most widely used in Western civilization
to-day, and more appropriate shapes than his have still to be
discovered.

But long before Staffordshire made its contribution,
European potters elsewhere had found one successful avenue
of escape from the limitations of the clumsy medieval earthenware. Their worst obstacle was the lead-glaze, which in firing
became so fluid as to blot any decoration not painted in thick
'slip' pigments, normally of rather subdued colour. It was
from the Islamic countries, probably from Moorish Spain, that
they learnt of a superior, more stable glaze, that would take
painting in bright colours and at the same time offer a fine
opaque white ground. The essential ingredient was white
oxide of tin. The 'Hispano-Moresque' dish in Plate 28 is
painted in gold lustre with the nervously sensitive brushwork
and ramifying freedom of design proper to Islamic pottery,
though the heraldic griffon is actually Gothic. Such wares
were first successfully imitated in Italy during the fifteenth

[44]

century. But painting on the Italian tin-glazed ware (so-called 'maiolica') soon took on the forms of the European Renaissance (Plate 29), and eventually the painting was considered more important than the pot it covered. From Italy the manufacture of similar painted wares spread to most European countries, including Britain (frontispiece), and until the second half of the eighteenth century, under the names of faïence or delftware, it remained the most popular kind of fine pottery. Its whole point lay in the painting (Plate 30), which was often so excellent as to excuse the comparative clumsiness of shape resulting from the thickness of the glaze and the softness of the clay it covered. But tin-glazed ware has now been obsolete for a century and a half. When treated to imitate porcelain (e.g. Plate 31) it became perilously brittle, and the cheaper and more serviceable hard white wares of Wedgwood type easily drove it off the market.

The nature of imported Chinese porcelain had baffled the researches of European potters for more than a century before its secret was independently rediscovered by a German chemist, at Meissen in Saxony, in the year 1709. Gradually the secret leaked out and other factories sprang up to rival Meissen. In France and England was introduced a glassy 'soft-paste' substitute for porcelain, which gave richer colour-effects when painted, but was clumsier to model. The vogue of porcelain in Europe first reached its height with the rococo style, whose tormented shapes and asymmetrical ornament it was peculiarly suited to express (Plates 32, 33, and 34). Extravagant modelling, jewel-like colour, and minutely delicate over-glaze painting are the very genius of European porcelain; it is a medium charged with such high potentialities that the frugal taste and timid craftsmanship of the present day can no longer do it justice.

17

19A

19B

20

22

23

26A

26B

28

29

30

31

32

33

5

Modern Wares

IN the countries of western civilization we seem to have stabilized the kinds of pottery we need for daily use. For the table we have either white earthenware of the Wedgwood type (and the Wedgwood factory is still one of the most progressive in England); or else the more expensive and durable white porcelain. Both are produced in great quantity, with all the resources of the modern chemist and engineer. And though, as anyone can see who visits an up-to-date factory, a surprising number of operations remain to be performed by the skilful human hand, this skill must all conform with a pattern worked out by a master-designer on his drawing-board. As a result we have wares whose technical perfection is virtually complete. It is in shapes and decoration, where style should be most eloquent, that we now seem tongue-tied. The nineteenth century revived the ornament of all previous ages. In table-wares, its especial delight was to reproduce by mechanical means the showy effects of eighteenth-century rococo porcelain. Since the First World War most people of taste have come to despise these ostentatious shams, and, after a brief but disastrous flirtation with 'modernistic' post-cubist art in the nineteen-twenties, have tried to re-establish a link with the style of the late eighteenth century. We now find the economy and elegance of late Georgian architecture very sympathetic, and our useful pottery often recalls, if it does not actually reproduce, the forms created by the first Josiah Wedgwood. But his slightly sentimental grace escapes

E

us. Even the simplest border-pattern painted on old 'Queen's ware' had a fragile life, hardly to be revived in a generation where everyone can write but few can draw. Hand-painting is at a discount with the modern industrialist, a brake on speed in production. Apart from shapes, our chief hope for aesthetic satisfaction lies in the use of new glazes, in new combinations of coloured materials, and in transfer-printing of contemporary design (Plate 36). Only in a few places on the European continent does 'porcelain-painting' still mean something in everyday speech (Plate 37).

A reaction against the mechanical and monotonous efficiency of modern industrial pottery began before the end of the nineteenth century, and in recent years a small number of 'studio-potters', working precariously as experimental craftsmen, have tried to broaden contemporary appreciation of pottery as an art. In England they have drawn inspiration from early Chinese stonewares, Japanese peasant-pottery, and old English slipware (Plates 38 and 39). So long as we continue to use polished wooden furniture and metal cutlery their productions cannot compete economically with our flimsy but convenient white crockery. They might at most grace the table in the country cottage where the weary seek refuge from urban civilization. But as objects of contemplation, the best 'studio' pots have a dignity and character that stand outside time and place (Plate 41); they are true works of art; and the imagination and skill of their making may even rouse an echo among the industrialists. It is significant that in some factory-made ornamental pottery we should now find matt, soft-toned glazes, and forms suggested by ancient bronze vessels from China (Plate 40).

35

36

37

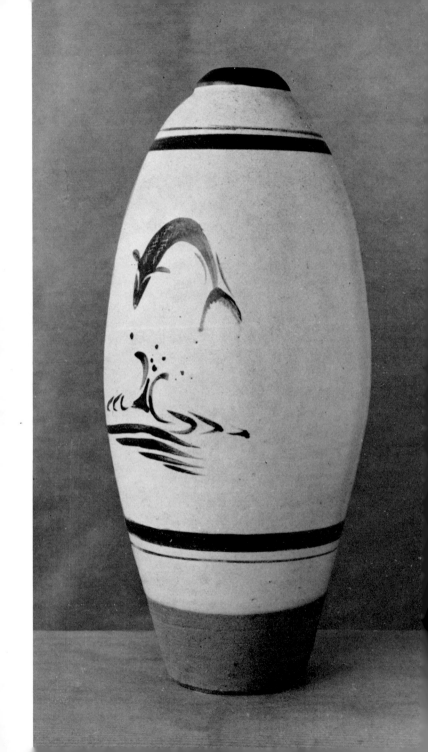

39

40

41

Notes on Plates

(*frontispiece*) Dish, tin-glazed earthenware painted in high-temperature colours. ENGLAND (LIVERPOOL); about 1760. W. 13 in. *Victoria and Albert Museum.*

I. The Ancient World

1. Storage-jar, buff earthenware painted in brown-black. From NEHAVAND (PERSIA). About 3000–2500 B.C. H. 23¾ in. *British Museum.*

2. Bottle, black burnished earthenware. From near DAMGHAN (PERSIA). About 3000 B.C. H. 9⅜ in. *Victoria and Albert Museum.*

3. Bowl, buff earthenware, painted in black, purple, and white. Ancient PERU (NASCA); perhaps 3rd century A.D. H. 4 in. *British Museum.*

4. Jug, buff earthenware painted in brown-black. GREECE (ATHENS); 8th century B.C. H. 16½ in. *Toronto, Royal Ontario Museum.*

5. Wine-jar (*amphora*), orange-red earthenware painted in black-figure style by Exekias. Memnon and two Ethiop squires. GREECE (ATHENS); about 530 B.C. H. 16½ in. *British Museum.*

6A, B. Cup (*kylix*), orange-red earthenware painted in black-figure style by Exekias. Dionysus sailing. GREECE (ATHENS); about 540–530 B.C. W. 11¾ in. *Munich, Antikensammlungen.*

7A. Jar, earthenware with black ground and trailed-on white clay ornament. ROMAN-BRITISH (CASTOR); 2nd–3rd century A.D. H. 4 $\frac{8}{10}$ in. *British Museum.*

7B. Cup, earthenware with green and deep yellow glazes. ROMAN-EGYPTIAN; 1st century B.C. or A.D. H. 2¾ in. *Victoria and Albert Museum.*

[74]

2. *The Near East*

8. Beaker, white ware. PERSIA; second half of 12th century. H. 5⅝ in. *Victoria and Albert Museum.*

9A, B. Bowl, white ware painted in black and pale blue under clear glaze. PERSIA (KASHAN); early 13th century. W. 7¾ in. *Victoria and Albert Museum.*

10A, B. Dish, white ware painted in black under clear glaze. PERSIA; second half of 12th century. W. 8⅛ in. *Victoria and Albert Museum.*

11. Jug, white ware painted in blue, grey, and purple under clear glaze. TURKEY (ISNIK); first half of 16th century. H. 12⅝ in. *Victoria and Albert Museum.*

12. Dish, white ware painted in colours under clear glaze. PERSIA; about 1600. W. 13½ in. *Formerly Kelekian Collection.*

3. *The Far East*

13. Reddish stoneware jar, with olive-grey glaze. CHINA; 3rd–4th century A.D. H. 13⅛ in. *Victoria and Albert Museum.*

14. Stoneware ewer, with olive-green glaze over scored lines. CHINA; 8th–9th century. H. 5½ in. *Victoria and Albert Museum.*

15. Earthenware vase with green glaze. CHINA (Sung period); A.D. 960–1279. H. 12$\frac{9}{16}$ in. *British Museum.*

16. Porcellaneous stoneware vase, with design carved under a green glaze ('Northern celadon'). CHINA; 12th–13th century. H. 9½ in. *Victoria and Albert Museum.*

17. Stoneware bottle, with design cut through a dark-brown glaze. CHINA (T'zü-chou); with date corresponding to A.D. 1305. H. 10 in. *British Museum.*

18. Stoneware vase, painted in brown on white ground under clear glaze. CHINA (T'zu-chou); 12th–13th century. H. 15½ in. *Victoria and Albert Museum.*

19A, B. Ewer and basin, white porcelain with bluish glaze. CHINA; 12th–13th century. H. of ewer 8$\frac{10}{16}$ in. *British Museum.*

20.   Stem-cup, white porcelain, painted in underglaze crimson. CHINA; mark and period of Emperor Hüsan Tê (1426–35). H. 4 in. *Victoria and Albert Museum.*

21.   Vase, porcelain painted with green, purple and white enamels on a pale yellow ground. CHINA; period of K'ang Hsi (1662–1722). H. 10¼ in. *Victoria and Albert Museum.*

22.   Bowl, porcelain painted in brilliant enamel colours, by the Kakiyemon family of Arita. JAPAN; about 1700. W. 5 ¹³⁄₁₆ in. *British Museum.*

23.   Tea-pot, red unglazed stoneware. CHINA (YI-HSING near SHANGHAI); late 17th century. H. 3¼ in. *Victoria and Albert Museum.*

4. *Pre-industrial Europe*

24.   Unglazed stoneware tankard. GERMANY (SIEGBURG, RHINE-LAND); late 15th century. H. 10¾ in. *Victoria and Albert Museum.*

25A, B. Loving-cup and dish, earthenware decorated in coloured clay 'slip' under a clear glaze. ENGLAND; late 17th century. H. of cup 4¼ in. W. of dish 13¾ in. *Victoria and Albert Museum.*

26A.   (*right to left*) Tankard, earthenware with dark-brown lead-glaze; cup, salt-glazed stoneware, brown at the top; tankard, unglazed red stoneware. ENGLAND; late 17th-early 18th century. H. 3½, 2½, and 3¾ in. *Victoria and Albert Museum.*

26B.   Tea-pot in red and white clay, with clear yellowish glaze. ENGLAND (STAFFORDSHIRE); about 1755. H. 4¾ in. *Victoria and Albert Museum.*

27.   Jug, salt-glazed white stoneware painted over the glaze in colours. ENGLAND (STAFFORDSHIRE); about 1750. H. 6½ in. *Victoria and Albert Museum.*

28.   Reverse of tin-glazed earthenware dish, painted in lustre with an heraldic griffon. HISPANO-MORESQUE (MANISES near VALENCIA); about 1450. W. 17 in. *Victoria and Albert Museum.*

29. Tin-glazed earthenware dish, painted in dark blue and white on a pale blue ground, showing Hercules and Antaeus. ITALY (VENICE); about 1540. W. 9½ in. *Victoria and Albert Museum.*

30. Dish, tin-glazed earthenware painted in blue with purple outlines. FRANCE (MARSEILLES, Saint Jean du Désert factory); about 1700. W. 22½ in. *Victoria and Albert Museum.*

31. Plate, tin-glazed earthenware. FRANCE (MARSEILLES); about 1765. W. 9¾ in. *Victoria and Albert Museum.*

32. Teapot, hard-paste porcelain. ITALY (LE NOVE); about 1765. H. 5¼ in. *Victoria and Albert Museum.*

33. Tea-pot, hard-paste porcelain. GERMANY (HÖCHST); about 1760. H. 4 in. *Victoria and Albert Museum.*

34. Vase and stand, soft-paste porcelain, painted in colours and gold, dark-blue ground. ENGLAND (CHELSEA); about 1765. H. 17 in. *Formerly R. W. M. Walker Collection.*

35. Chocolate-cup and stand, cream-coloured earthenware. ENGLAND (Wedgwood); about 1790. H. of cup 4 in. *Victoria and Albert Museum.*

5. Modern Wares

36. Jug and bowl, white earthenware with printed decoration designed by ERIC RAVILIOUS. ENGLAND (Wedgwood); about 1938. H. of jug 8½ in. *Victoria and Albert Museum.*

37. White earthenware plate and sauce-boat, painted in underglaze colours. Designed by NILS THORSSON. DENMARK (Aluminia branch of the Royal Copenhagen Porcelain Factory); about 1938. W. of plate 9⅜ in. *Victoria and Albert Museum.*

38. Stoneware vase painted in brown on a cream-white ground. Made by BERNARD LEACH at ST. IVES, CORNWALL, about 1930. H. 12⅞ in. *Collection of the Dean of York.*

39. Stoneware bowl painted in brown. Made in ENGLAND by STAITE MURRAY about 1930. W. 7¼ in. *Collection of the Dean of York.*

[77]

40. Vase, white earthenware with matt ivory glaze. Designed by KEITH MURRAY; made by Wedgwood's about 1936. H. 7¼ in. *Victoria and Albert Museum.*

41. Dish, red earthenware painted with zircon glazes in 'inlay and overlay' technique, by JOYCE MORGAN. ENGLAND (LONDON, Chelsea Pottery); 1953. W. 7⅜ in. *Victoria and Albert Museum.*

Plates 3, 7A, 9B, 15, 17, and 22 are from photographs taken by Fine Art Engravers, Ltd.; Plates 38 and 39 from photographs by Mr. W. J. Green of York. The remainder, except Plates 1 and 26A, are from official photographs of the Victoria and Albert Museum, the British Museum, the Royal Ontario Museum of Art and Archaeology, and the Antikensammlungen, Munich, as named in the accompanying descriptions. The publishers wish to thank the authorities of the museums for giving facilities to publish objects in their charge.

Index

Britain, Roman, 26, *Plate 7A*

Chelsea, 17, *Plate 34*
Chinese pottery, 12, 29, 41–2, *Plates 13–21, 23*; decoration of, 17, 41–2; influence of, 11, 27, 41–2, 43, 45, 66
clay, 12, 14–15, 20, 27, 29, 45
colour, 13–14, 20, 25, 45

decoration, 14, 17–19, 20, 25, 45; Chinese, 17, 41–2; Greek, 25–26; modern, 66; Persian, 27–8, 41; slip, 43
delftware, 45
Denmark, 66, *Plate 37*
dishes, 18

earthenware, 12–13, 20, 25, 65
Egypt, 20, 26, *Plate 7B*
England, 17, 26, 43–5, 65–6, *Frontispiece, Plates 25–7, 34–6, 38–41; and see* Britain, Roman
Exekias, *Plates 5, 6*

Faience, 45
firing of pottery, 13–14
France, 43, *Plates 30, 31*

Germany, 43, 45, *Plates 24, 33*
glaze, 13–14, 20, 25–6, 29, 43–5, 66; lead, 13, 43–4; salt, 13, 43, 44; tin, 44–5
Gothic style, 43, 44
Greek pottery, 20, *Plates 4–6*;

decoration of, 17, 25–6; influence of, 44

Islamic pottery, *see* Persia; Spain; Turkey
Italy, 44–5, *Plates 29, 32*

Japan, 66, *Plate 22*

Leach, Bernard, *Plate 38*
lead-glaze, 13, 43–4
Liverpool, *Frontispiece*

majolica, 45
Meissen, 45
modern wares, 15, 65–6
Morgan, Joyce, *Plate 41*
moulds, use of, 15
Murray, Keith, *Plate 40*
Murray, Staite, *Plate 39*

ornament, *see* decoration
oxides, 13

Persian pottery, 14, 20, 25–6, 27–8, *Plates 1, 2, 8–10, 12*; decoration of, 20, 27–8, 41; influence of, 43–4
Peru, 25, *Plate 3*
pigment, *see* colour
porcelain, 12–14, 45, 65
'punctuation', 17–18

Queen's ware, 44, 66

[79]